Cadabra

THE DREAMSEEKER POETRY SERIES

Books in the DreamSeeker Poetry Series, intended to make available fine writing by Anabaptist-related poets, are published by Cascadia Publishing House under the DreamSeeker Books imprint and often copublished with Herald Press. Cascadia oversees content of these poetry collections in collaboration with the DreamSeeker Poetry Series Editor Jeff Gundy (Jean Janzen volumes 1-4) as well as in consultation with its Editorial Council and the authors themselves.

1. On the Cross
   By Dallas Wiebe, 2005
2. I Saw God Dancing
   By Cheryl Denise, 2005
3. Evening Chore
   By Shari Wagner, 2005
4. Where We Start
   By Debra Gingerich, 2007
5. The Coat Is Thin, 2008
   By Leonard Neufeldt
6. Miracle Temple, 2009
   By Esther Stenson
7. Storage Issues, 2010
   By Suzanne Miller
8. Face to Face, 2010
   By Julie Cadwallader-Staub
9. What's in the Blood, 2012
   By Cheryl Denise
10. The Apple Speaks, 2012
    By Becca J. R. Lachman

11 Momentary Stay, 2015
    By Barbara Esch Shisler
12 What the Body Knows, 2015
    By Jean Janzen
13 Cadabra, 2015
    By Jen Kindbom

Also worth noting are two poetry collections that would likely have been included in the series had it been in existence then:

1 Empty Room with Light
   By Ann Hostetler, 2002
2 A Liturgy for Stones
   By David Wright, 2003

DreamSeeker Books also continues to release occasional high-caliber collections of poems outside of the DreamSeeker Poetry Series:

1 The Mill Grinds Fine: Collected Poems
   By Helen Wade Alderfer, 2009
2 How Trees Must Feel
   By Chris Longenecker, 2011

Cadabra

poems by
Jen Kindbom

DreamSeeker Poetry Series, Volume 13

DreamSeeker Books
TELFORD, PENNSYLVANIA

an imprint of
Cascadia Publishing House LLC

Cascadia Publishing House orders, information, reprint permissions:
contact@CascadiaPublishingHouse.com
1-215-723-9125
126 Klingerman Road, Telford PA 18969
www.CascadiaPublishingHouse.com

Cadabra
Copyright © 2015 by Cascadia Publishing House LLC
All rights reserved
DreamSeeker Books is an imprint of Cascadia Publishing House LLC
Library of Congress Catalog Number: 2014043473
ISBN 13: 978-1-68027-003-7
Book design by Cascadia Publishing House
Cover design by Gwen M. Stamm

The paper used in this publication is recycled and meets the
minimum requirements of American National Standard for Information
Sciences—Permanence of Paper for Printed Library Materials, ANSI Z39.48-1984.1984

Versions of poems in this collection have appeared in various outlets.
For a complete listing, see Acknowledgments and Credits section, back
of book.

Library of Congress Cataloguing-in-Publication Data
Kindbom, Jen.
 [Poems. Selections]
 Cadabra : poems / Jen Kindbom.
  pages cm. -- (Dreamseeker Poetry Series; Volume 13)
 Summary: "As it highlights home, including in Ohio, Cadabra invokes creating through speaking what is magical and ordinary, what is home and observable, what potential lies in what's waiting"-- Provided by publisher.
 ISBN 978-1-68027-003-7 (5.5 x 8.5 trade pbk. : alk. paper)
 I. Title.
 PS3611.I5696A6 2015
 811'.6--dc23
                                2014043473

20 19 18 17 16 15   10 9 8 7 6 5 4 3 2 1

For Kyle, of course, and Cole and Lilly—

and for K.M.B.—
thank you for the reminder.

TABLE OF CONTENTS

ONE

Lepidoptera • 15
Cadabra • 17
Typewriter Love Song • 18
Summer Turning • 20
In the dream she puts a note on the door • 21
Prayer Flags • 22
In the Cabinet Drawer • 23
Porch Day • 24
Lillian Ode • 26
Repair • 28
Caterpillar • 30
Love Bugs • 31
Market • 32
Flash Flood • 33
This One Birth • 34
Rainbow • 36
Deer Dog • 37
Books at Night • 38
Poem Row • 39

Moving Day • 41
Moon, Waving • 42

TWO

Mayfly Season • 45
In the Weeping Cherries • 46
Loved One • 47
A Kind of Haunting • 48
After The Fish • 50
Appetite • 51
Spider Bites • 52
Pepper Slice • 53
You are a souvenir • 54
Bluff Tree • 57
Rosary • 59
Alice • 60
Cemetery Road • 61
Startled: A Confession • 62
Vespers • 64
January 31 • 66
Highway Ode • 68
Goodbye, Darkness • 70
X-Ray • 72
Pitcher • 73
Love Poem • 75
Prayer • 76
Moth Exit • 78
Nocturnal Pine • 79

Road Chickens • 81
September Ivy • 82
Yes, this is a poem about— • 83
In Memory • 84
Neighbor Blessing • 85
Nearsighted • 86
Memorable You • 87

Acknowledgments 89
The Author 91

ONE

Lepidoptera

I am full of butterflies—
breathe in: they flutter in my nose,
land in my stomach and lungs,
my teeth and tongue and palate—

they land inside me, the
other side of my skin,
and uncoil their own long mouths,
nudging me—
they land behind my eyes,
stretch their antenna-arms,
their feather feet—

they fill me, my hands,
and they are fast—
my fingers buzz through
these pictures of you—
my bones are butterflies:
my blood, *sanguine papillon.*

I am full of butterflies—
an army of wing,
almost inaudible, but not—
see them fly from my ears,
my mouth. (I carry on.)

Come close:
they perch on me
and cover my eyes—

it is all chrysanthemum and sky.
I taste them, hear
their little words,
wing words, foot words, long words
of head and thorax—

they fill me, then
their damp wings stretch
into the light—
I am their cocoon, stretching
my own hand to them,

and they land there too.
They are me, I am them—

Cadabra

I invent you:
your turns of line
translate in a sunless spot
into turns of hand,
curves of face, of foot—
I invent your
hair and tone, both quiet
but untamed like air.

When I read you,
I invent your heather shrug, those
fisherman pants you wear.
Like some wizard of fabrication,
I invent your schedule (busy but
guarded) and your friends
(garden-keeping types, vegetarians).

I've invented with my mind's shining wand
your home, every sanctuary,
your cupboards (plentiful but not
excessive) your floor (clean, but
not obsessively so). I have invented
a dog for you,
your fondness for him.

Your teeth and skin I've invented—
knees and nails, scents—
all of this a knitted fiction.

Typewriter Love Song

I scan the rows of junk
for the small black trunk, five bucks.

Now here we are,
me and the typing machine,
the Deluxe Noiseless Remington,
its elegant hardware.

On our way home, it
rides in the front seat.

I pull of its masking tape tag
and once we're home,
I tuck it in

and crawl in next to it.

It writes me good morning, hello—
it writes me breakfast and lunch.

It whispers,
asks if I remember the news.

I wind new paper,
and it writes me a fairy tale.

We awaken, and
there's a horse in the room,
a deep well, a ribbon of sky across the ceiling,
a pool of fish and a bucket of gold.

The typewriter sits in the window,
noiseless keys in the sun.

I hear it writing sometimes in the night,
about the flea market,
the night stand,
the news room, half a memoir.

Summer Turning

This is the year you turned in the summer
and tomorrow they'll cut you down.

Tonight, enjoy the bulbous mushroom
that you hold in the curve of your arm like a drum.

Wake the cardinals and squirrels, and
drum, mild oak, in the red moon
of your too-early leaves.

Forget your are dead—
forget you are logs and rusty chips
before noon—

Wake us all instead:
move us to our windows
on this, your last night.

Call to us until the bulbs burn
and no eye is dry,

until the soil hums and rocks on its muddy heels—

call until the sun comes up
and the trucks arrive.

In the dream she puts a note on the door

saying she found fourteen dollars in the pocket of her coat.
It is pencil and typing paper, addressed to the neighbors,
taped there in the hallway.

Delivery to this old apartment
with the curving, loud river rushing by just under the window
        sill—
maybe four inches under it—would cost too much and take too
        long.

A small wild possum jumps in through the window
        eats with slow, small bites the champagne-pink grapes
that shine in the sun in a shell-pearl bowl. It runs.

We bathe, my belly floating in the tub—hers tiny, invisible.

Desks line up in the parking garage—they will be towed soon.

She has lived here two years. I try to access my waking
knowledge to see if it's really been that long.
There's a tin rose on the table,
those jewel grapes shining like mad—

I reach for the telephone, and she tells me it's time—we
lace our boots
and bolt the door.

Prayer Flags

The prayers are flying down the street

flying
down the street

Flying from the tree where they wave
onto the man whose hair stands up
and onto the white dog who walks at his side

onto the mail carrier and
the heavy bag of mail he carries,
his face away from the wind,
onto his shoulders, prayers flying,

flying,
sticking to the prayer-wet windows, prayers,
sticking then sliding, and praying.

Their colors have become little fogs,
whispering red, blue, yellow, green.
Their letters too are whispers in fog.

Prayer flags praying
praying till they're just prayers and string

then just the smoke and burning string
then just prayers
flying.

In the Cabinet Drawer

How can I name the smell
in the drawer of the thrift store sewing machine?

It is her breath,
the breath of her dress form,
dress—

her belly, breathing her first child,
second—

cool breath of slow clay earth
beneath her feet, swing
where she held them—

breath of wind and the skirt
holding,

and in the hot exhale of summer,
sliding to the floor—

Porch Day

Neighbor I know only as neighbor
tells me I remind her
of her mother on Sundays, scrubbing the porch
early in her dress and morning hair,
rivers across the planks to the spindles,
dew on the grass, suds—*She wore pink,
had champagne hair—*

Little black rivers race down the house,
seasons of pollen and dirt from the road—
This place hasn't been washed in years.

The Edmiston place, the Nickel place,
the Amerine place, the Morgan place,
the Kindbom place.

I scrub the wooden siding with a cloth
and chase a dime-sized spider from a corner—
she hides on the underside
of a board
and I leave her—
this is her place as much as mine. *She
let the water run—her elbows, down her sides—
she sang, most days—*

When I rinse again,
another slick of mud rolls to the floor,
rolls onto the ceiling,
rains onto me. *Mother lifted*

*clover from down the yard into her apron,
gave it to her daughter, who fed it to the rabbit—*

It dries slowly—still early—
making peaks of wet
along cracked paint lines.

Lillian Ode

your birth hair
falls away like the copper beams of an old day
and new locks replace it, painted all
hay and peaches

I could live forever with my nose to your head—

*

here on this vast shelf of the start of your life
you are poised—

you seem to memorize something—
this room, my face, the width of cotton beneath your head—

to pull upon this early knowledge later,
after it grows and takes my place—
you will rise, still poised,
into the world—

*

brand new tears
that flow all around your head
when I must tend to your brother's bath

your soft nails that peel so easily, like cellophane

your reflexive hug that grips the gift bear from your grandfather

your gaping gummy smile,
all for me in the morning—

*

come with me, child,
bundled in blanket and hat,
and see the snow—

with such little discretion
it lights lightly on the lawn

shines the table of stump—

see—it wraps its palm around the other trees, Lilly,
presses its hand onto the roofs of houses and garages
who lean into and away from it—

see it land, a cloak on our backs
lingering a moment—

Repair

Spiders like little knots of hair hurry out from blistered paint I
    scrape away;
doubling back, I see my own blood on the siding wood.

The house's skin becomes mine, flakes and specks and
    scrapes—
Five-in-one between the planks, and toothy shims rain down
    from the huge gaps—
I suspect they were keeping this place from caving in on itself,
under its thousand layers of heat and paint and blood and
    lead—

There's a roach in a web, amber, dangling—
dead daisies under the tarp—
I'm entirely too contemplative for the occasion.
The spiders are the ones whose houses I'm scraping away—
silent apologies, it must be done.

They scurry and lurk as I slice along the boards,
their old spent sacks,
new ones with a girth of life—
some gray dirt, some dusty decay—
we'll wash away.

Every ancient nail I see is loose,
except the ones that really matter.
Isn't that how it goes—
another streak of blood,
another puff of dust.

I open and reopen the skin of my knuckles.

Caterpillar

You press my mind
toward childhood
and fancy love

and so I don't think
about the wash
of your ghostly
waiting wing

or how
so suddenly,

as we dance our
nightmarish dance
in the cast light
of the porch,

its shroud will trip
the bare skin
of my arm.

Love Bugs

They say that only humans and dolphins
experience pleasure in sex

but after these Japanese beetles today
I'm not so sure—

They've consumed the sweet tent of a broad leaf
leaving only its brown lace for their embrace,
all iridescent exoskeleton.

They dance their stacked shuffle
in the bed between the two sidewalks,
devouring it as they go.

Some quiver—exhausted—already alone.
Others pile up,
swaying with the watching wind,

pronged middle legs arching up to the sky,
front and back ones desperately gripping their love.

Market

Today, it is four degrees
and people mill about
rows and rows of
sausage and pasta, liver and ribs,
beautiful bricks of bread
and pierogi in drums—

people passing and milling
the market's grid of vendor cases.

I was eight perhaps, or seven
and it was open-air then—
a pretzel, giant lemonade,
red straw—

produce house, comfort station.

The Market's tiled, Byzantine ceiling
is the great palm of the city
cupping over us all in this moment:

gusts rushing 25th like quick fingers,
a bench of observers,
a slab of salmon, whole,
silvery eye on ice.

Flash Flood

The grass lies down where the sky,
like a hound,
has licked its watery wounds.

Mud bubbles and crawls,
blood in the quick of the nail.

The blind beast-flood prowls and slows,
sliding its belly in the ditch
then the walk
then the road and concrete stair.

It finds the earth-slick path
beyond the basement panes
into the house,

into drawers and photographs,
unfolding and imprinting, strewing
with its wet paw.

When it can no longer reach or climb,
it shudders and puddles in the corner,
makes a whimper before it dries.

This One Birth

We are both in tears, little one,
your pushing and kicking and weight
and waiting,
such throbbing—

you are five now,
three nurses restrain you
and I hold your face to mine—

> *three hours of pushing*
> *then cutting*
> *then exhaustion,*
> *heat lamps—*

you flail your forty pounds,
and I cannot lift you—
a nurse stands stunned,
as if this is the first
she's witnessed
a birth of this nature.

Momentary reprieve—then
you wail, your homelust
tearing through the building—
my face to yours,
now tears, only pools—

only a printed flannel blanket holds you,
just eight pounds of you,
infant fuzz, infant voice—

then, full moon breasts, heavy—
new marks, permanent—
this one birth,
and then another.

This is as good as I've got—
as good as you've got, little one,

and it's good, under the sun of everything,
this pulling and pushing,
our dancing forever.

Rainbow

This strange place on the edge of weather
allows simultaneous rain and sun

simultaneous rain and sun
here where the sun's the same time as the rain

the edge of weather
edge of weather with sun and rain
a corridor—only door and air and light

a corridor of buildings of painted brick
rainbow buildings who line the street
of the edge of weather

who hold up the ribbon sky
mortar and baked edges, painted—
the edge of weather

sun and rain simultaneous
a rainbow street, a corridor, just door
holding houses whose bricks hold the sky.

Deer Dog

I've been reading about
the delicate lips of deer in winter
and the cranberries they softly mouthe.

Now it is summer, and
in the dog's purple mouth, water
quickly turns to strands
and dangles on his lips.

Would the cranberry deer,
do you suppose,
come to our yard
and show him how to be delicate—

dip their berry lips into the pool
nod, and shoot glances
toward the old dog, their pupil?

Or would they watch him
and sneaking, tag each of us
with purple, purple!

Books at Night

At night these books are wild.
And watch!—the street light sneaks in
and startles them all awake—
a feral shuffling of pages
and arching of spines.

You can hear them in their case—listen!—
trading secrets and plotting together,
becoming just one book and then a hundred,
taking small flights between each shelf
and never whispering   *the end.*

They flit from shelf to shelf
scratching the gravel, tripping through the night
with wide wings and black eyes
and long tales—

Dawn comes, and they tuck their pages
away like feathers.
Until dusk, they bury their word-beaks
again in the stacks.

Poem Row
for Joey

Would you take this path
paved in glowing pronoun
lighted with metaphor
lined with benches like stanza
and little dashes that bloom
through the cobbled iambs?

Stop and feed the similes—
toss them broken dactyls
and lines—
see them flutter around
the refrain of your footsteps.

Meet me in the shade of
the tree, outstretching, calling   *tree—*

Under the echo of that echo,
let us place our place
in the soft grass of assonance.

Let us pull the pennants from the porches
and wrap our words in them—

Let us drink from tiny couplets
and spread enjambment on our toast—

cut me off with a mad dash
or let me run on
and on
our pronoun path,
our word-lit road.

Moving Day
for Al

I don't want your plague of dying cats
or wasps like thunder under the siding,

your pocket doors that dangle
or your roof of jittery holes.

I don't want your double-hung windows,
cross-eyed and hexed with no weights or ropes

or the sneaky ghost who swoops your stairs
to frighten the cats for fun.

I do not want your thousand spiders
who tiptoe the ceiling,

your jig-sawed crown moulding
whose gaps gape like wicked absent teeth.

Your drafts, creaky peaks,
all of your un-square footage—

somebody will relish in your abundant fodder,
but leaning house, it isn't me.

Moon, Waving

Tonight it could be the bulb
I left burning down in the hall
in the kitchen—

it waves itself over the trees
which wave themselves over the snow,
which is waves—

I might wake the boy,
carry him to the window—
after three sleepless years, wake him—

your moon,   I might say,
and then his echo,   *my moon,*
remembering for a minute,
not remembering.

I will climb the blue stairs
where the moon throws itself.
Stairs creak and I might
wake the moon, too, if it slept—

and I might wake it,
saying   *look, look—*

TWO

Mayfly Season

and they are the backdrop
for everything.

Empty bodies
form a flannel
that floats atop Lake Erie.

The ones who surround this pier
catch your eye—

before you realize it
wings are the air
and the words between us.

In the Weeping Cherries
There are people
in the weeping cherries

sweeping the street
with the cuffs of their pants,

greeting each other
with nods and snaps.

I see them,
neighbors tripping along
when light is just that way,

when the air
fills their airy hands,
moves them so.

When I look directly,
they are gone—

leafy limbs
and all,
run, run away.

Loved One

In my mind
I tended the earth there
with a shovel and your gloves.

I made you a garden of zinnias
and morning glories,
peonies to bloom for you in June.

I cleared away grass that bends and bows,
the creeping charlie's tangled fingers,
spent vines from the season before.

I recycled the cans and wrappers

and against your monument,
harder than countertop, colder,

I have leaned to catch the snow that falls,
to feel the sun that shines where you are.

A Kind of Haunting

The lake gobbled up the center of town—

the buoy, bending and bobbing, could be
a girl, bending
to touch her knee, the waves,

the place where—after cholera—
the poor bodies were tossed,

bending down in the center of town.

The buoy is the ghost of a girl
before Lake Erie gobbled up the square,
before cholera led the bodies to the water,
then to the shore—

She wades to her knees in water over her head,
washing her arms in the center of town—
tall windows of the Piety Hill castles,
shadows of Williams Street.

The Old Plat is left, the hungry lake's left it alone,
gurgling gravel, warm August tide that can't freeze
but does—then creaks and moans till spring
and the buoys wiggle free again.

She only bends, never dives, only dips
her hair, only wets again her wet breast,
this ghost at the center of town—

this dusky sand as the night comes up,
and she could be me,
she could be you—
a girl ghost in the center of town—
before the square, sidewalk, gazebo, carriage,
pedestrians all at the bottom—
twenty-four feet down and halfway to Canada—

She holds a mirror in the west basin—
holds it and turns it, a different lens—

The sun comes and she's still there—she'll turn
and wave   and wave

and wave
from the center of town.

After the Fish

Oh Elizabeth,
it is still rainbow,
rainbow, rainbow—
the bilge on the parking lot, and
now, the sand—
we still throw the fish back; we
etch our names on the cold ground
and pull our hands away,
turn our eyes toward what's lighter—

It is still rainbow:
our tremendous tasks are the hooks
in our tender jaws. We throw ourselves
back again and again, we fill
with air—
we float to the surface, we drive away—
our rainbows stay,
this bizarre and clouded print of life.

The green grows up around us, Elizabeth,
and we wait, the peonies of our hearts exploding,
our irises, too, still—

Would you cast your line again? Entangle us
in your ancient ribbons.

Appetite

Airport absorbed edges of neighborhood:
houses are gone but yards and drives remain.
Somehow the grass stays short,
mown by ghosts of bulldozed bungalows.

Houses are gone, but neat square yards remain
up and down Forestwood and Midvale Avenues,
mown by ghosts of bulldozed bungalows
beyond barriers at the top of the street.

Up and down Avenues where friends lived
the ghosts weave in and out where windows were
beyond barriers at the top of the street,
along sidewalks where nobody walks.

The ghosts weaving where windows were—
we watch them when we come back again
to sidewalks where nobody walks
along the edge where Hopkins stopped.

We watch them again when we come back.
Somehow the grass stays short
along the edge where the airport ends,
the neighborhood edge that Hopkins absorbed.

Spider Bites
Last night
I was visited by
the ghost of the spider I killed.

His gauzy folded legs floated up
from the crypt of under-the-bed

and carried him, spinning and spinning,
supernatural arachnid flotsam.

Here he did his worst.

In the bathroom mirror
I find his vapor bites,
slight and pale,

which spell in eight-armed shorthand
across my face,
See you tonight.

Pepper Slice

When I slice the smooth face off a pepper
another one appears,
a craggy gap, dangling seed teeth.

I peer into the growling jaw

and it widens, more fearful now,
fierce stalactites.

Knife drips with the juice from the scaly pulp inside,
trembles with light and dark on the blade.

The sound is like paper on itself
and it is only its core now,
a chasm, a maw with its head of teeth, ghoulish
and too heavy for the soft, sunless skeleton.

You are a souvenir
a returning moon,
shaking off the emptiness
then generating it again—

I am tethered to you, empty vessel.

*

If I had known, there's a chance
I would've pulled myself
from that tub
and draped a gown around my body and,
bulging with an almost born bag of life,
gone fleeing to a sweeter sanctuary:

Instead of maternity nurses discussing
postpartum, my body, Pitocin,

I'd lean
on the ladder of a tree house
and rock
and the hot waves of labor
would wash over me—

no doors, I would howl and lower myself down
into a tumbling stream, where I'd stay,
swaddled with current until the moment
of my own waters' bursting—

then I'd weave a basket from water and cotton
and hyacinth, and in that final fire
and push, I'd catch her in it.

And then, as her lips would draw her first air and
I would fill with her first meal,
and as you, that vacant vessel, would wring yourself
of her habitat,
we would rest in tall grass—we would swing
in a fashioned hammock between two trees.

*

I pull my naked self from the teeming pool, effacement,
dilation, half-sitting under lights.
You take over. The doctor urges *wait*, the nurse urges *wait*
but I cannot—we cannot—and I wail—
Her precious head is out, my grandmother's face—
and then her cord and feet—
perfection, then placenta.

*

Rest, and globs of blood, then kneading—
like knives and shovels tearing out the soft remains—
head nurse who won't explain,
won't concede, won't introduce herself:
forearm to fiery canal—

*

I will carry you like beach glass, like a river stone
in a pocket, the thumb of my memory fixed forever
to some figment of you.

Bluff Tree

Prophecy

The time will come when you may no longer come to me.
(I will still dangle my finger-branches into the valley,
I will still embrace the bridge and slate,
I will hold the sky.)

You will leave the dappled ants again forever—
the time is coming—
you will rest your soft body
against the ridges and root-bowls of mine again never.

My earth floor will start to drop away—
tiny crumbs and broken wafers of slate at first,
then rocks, then boulders of earth
until I myself am the sheer drop,
the sheer drop's edge.

Walls and fences and signs will come,
and the drop of my silver leaf and reflection
against the spot that used to be you
will fall into the listening air instead.

You will come to the river
and immerse yourself in the lines of my reflection—
lay yourself down, your hands holding the sky,
catching the tiny slate that rolls down the edge.

Note

Seems the last time we touched
was the last time we'd touch—
the sisters have built a fence and posted a sign.

Tree, it's not your fault
that the ground you grip
won't grip you in return. Don't be
alarmed when your roots feel the air of the valley
instead of the mud and slate.

Tell the ants and silver leaves
that I would come back if I could—
my soft self in the bowls of your roots—
and while their shadows paraded over me, I'd feed them
my thoughts and crumbs.

Tree, maybe I will steal away to you again
in the cover of shadowy night
behind the convent and the leaning graves,
over the new fence

tiptoe the sinking ground,
the two of us, our fingers
to the cool valley.

Rosary

What I do with the wrist rosary my mother brings me from your house after you die is complicated because of the brassy links between the Hail Marys. You said Our Lady of Somewhere reached down and touched them and that's why their silver plate turned to brass—and so at fourteen, I don't know what is an appropriate thing to do with this relic of you,

this relic whose plastic purple beads have gone to white at the edges and seams.

I hang it on the corner of a shadowbox for a while, up on the wall with the ceramic animals. It will be safe here from earthly contamination and the floor. Then I put it in a box

and take it out now and then and remember you. I do this for nine years.

Now I'm grown, and I still don't know what to do with your rosary. How many have I had and lost? It is in my jewelry box, its worn beads and miracle brass—those silent beads

from which you squeezed so much God.

Alice

You have her winter eyes, I realize after a moment,
and her black hair
before it whispered to white.

You have her
stunning blue-white teeth.

Your voice is different
but your stance so familiar
that I'm remembering her before I know
I'm remembering:

the way she leaned on the counter
and the fibers of her peony sweater
shining in the kitchen's incandescence,
the smell of cucumber—

narrow elbows
and the exact angles of the bones of her face
before she was too gone to speak, to move—

and when you talk about feeling closeness
to a person you've never met,
I feel she's come to me again.

Cemetery Road

Wedged between corn and wetlands:
forgive me, my white knuckles, dear road,
your sealed and chipped curves,
your dark, dark curves—

I get away from myself here with you
studying so hard your length before me
for the next curve or an animal or buggy—
forgive me,
with you I am not myself.

Lamps find the monuments and bony trees
for which you are named
and I don't tarry there—
wonder if I'd like you more in the light—
forgive me.

Startled: A Confession

Out of vast nowhere,
here it comes—

a prickling of the neck
a certain quease at a creeping face-shadow
a voice in the roar of the toilet's flush
the photo-negative of all an off'd light's horrors
hidden in a blink

the inability not to ponder
every imagined danger
between the bathroom and the bed

that horrible ring of quietness
that awful darkness of the space
where the attic door didn't latch

light bulbs growing warm and their tiny terrible ticks
that raise bumps on the back of the hand

weird figures out of the corner of the eye

my own hair
sprawled in a dark, mandrakey mess,
all Hannibal Lector and Pennywise and
Carrie—

every night I meet these—
the stuff of a child's nightmares—

and that is why I like
for us to go to bed
together.

Vespers

You are a billion miles away

pruning the pear trees in the old garden,
or sipping green tea on a soft winding path,
whistling on the seventh day

as I thrash about
in what I've made
of what you've given me.

Give us silence
seems today too grand a request
though we pray also *give us peace*

and food for all of our hungers
and salvation and are satisfied—

What can I learn from this spinning, this long,
constant orbit of hallway to chair, creaking floor to
creaking runner?
How can your silence
be your answer?

Let me hear your still, small voice—
your still   small voice—

let it fill me again.

Turn from your pear trees
to my full, heavy arms

and touch your gift again.

January 31

and days are short
and this is not news to anyone—

the mind clings—
and fingers and hands cling
and faces and eyes and souls cling—
yes, souls—
fiercely
as dark to night—

they cling to every shaft of light,
even those shafts split from themselves,
split as winter selves are—
through thick trunks of gutter ice:

this part stays and writes the poem.
This part flies over tomorrow's highway—
no, the literal highway—
the same part that won't go into the dark
willingly,
that regards with hot suspicion
the periphery of vision
and ill-fitting spectacles—
same
permanent state of startled—
winter state of startled—
winter state.

The sky over that self
begins to crack
in January
and fall—
it is all an ice storm.

The thin beams
push themselves through glowing ice

and hands, chapped,
clinging.

Highway Ode

I am highway
under a pane of ice,
the long pane of snow.

I curl, all spine
and resistance,
under grumbling plows.

My skin cracks
then breaks
then fills with winter
and cracks again—

comes away in
pavement stones,
reveals giant bowls
of whatever's left,
flavorless salt.

I follow you—
no, you follow me—
no, I am highway.

Hand on my shoulder,
a ditch I can't reach.
You turn and turn back
and turn away,
one way,
that way.

I tremble when you're near—

crossing the berm,
median,
divider, divided—
double yellow
all lined way
high up
highway.

Goodbye, Darkness

I don't need you anymore.
You are not my hands or eyes,
my love or my pet.

Goodbye—
I'll put you in a bucket
and take you down
to the creek.

I'll open the door
of your wooden pen
and pat your haunch
till you scutter away.

I'll tap your shell with a stick
and tell you
you're free!
go home!

I'll take you to the other side
of the stream
where you'll lose my scent, whine,
and go your own way.

I'll forget to drop crunch nuggets
into your bowl,
and out of necessity, you will go—or

I'll slip the smooth needle
into your vein, and when
you've twitched and withered to sleep,
I'll send you off—

Goodbye darling darkness—
forget to write.

X-Ray

We peer
through the dusty window
into the hornet-filled cavity
of your chest.

It is spirograph and balls of wire,
a winding network of soggy tumors
that, until today, we could only suspect.

For the tired engine of your breath,
that last station is near:
the quick needle of sleep, your conductor.

You will leave us today,
and we will imagine you young,
a glistening dog of the sky

shaken free to pad the clouds—no leash
or gate or floor:

you will sit near a great window
at the foot of a master's great bed
and nudge his hand
as he stirs once more to pat your head.

Pitcher

When I smack the replacement glass pitcher into
the side of the sink and
it sings its song of not
breaking,
not yet—

when I can hear the molecules
sprinting around its wide hips
and up around its open lips, sprinting
like sand under a salty wave,
like salt drying away—

when I can see where the crack should be—
up through the stout neck, around the handle
whose strength leaves me stunned,
straight around the belly like an egg
and yet no crack appears—

when I slam the pitcher again from sheer clumsiness
and pull it back and I find no crack,
for a minute it is you—

it does not shatter into the drain (though it could),

it does not refuse to hold water (though it could),

it does not pinch my hand with fear
of what could have been its end
(though it certainly could).

It is fragile and strong,
thick and thin,
opaque and translucent, transparent

and if it could, it would hold me.

Love Poem

i.

Because you left the light on for me
I am more aware of the sound of myself—
my humid foot on the floor,
the air in my throat,
the rustling of my leg
within its pant—

even my thoughts are audible, I imagine,
and so I try to think quietly
into your sleep.

ii.

I wake cold in our bed
missing the broad brown leaf
of your back.

How strange,
even in this hot lung of summer,
to feel a chill.

I turn in the covers—

you're fast on your way,
a shot in the
almost-light.

Prayer

Stranger things have happened—
the Earth sputtering out from nothing,
benign creator's clay-crusted thumb
dug deep into the pit of it,
all of life gasping into light,
and light—

a road thick with butterflies—
they butter the air,
winging along, impossible tumbles
over the asphalt
and then an explosion of something—
here, now, or another here, now—

Stranger things have happened than life persisting,
finding beautiful white hair again
and twenty pounds and restful sleep—

We know all we know
is in the realm of the possible—
we turn like dough in a bowl,
like meringue, like the sky,
like bread clouds on a board—
all of these,
butterflies we dodge, that fill us—
all possible—

pneumonia flushing itself away,
hands back in the mud and trees,
back at the blade and the blocks,
health and youth—

These, and ten-ton trees that grow straight up
with no coaxing—

These, and my babies, born,
my belly expelling the blanket placenta—

These, and satellites to circle where
once, there was nothing,
footprints on a thing that was nothing once—

stranger has happened than rewinding,
than finding, removing, restoring, erasing, placing—
retroaction—

these, and how I even know you at all—

I put my prayer on the backs of butterflies
who fly in a jar and out again—

would you hold it to your lips.

Moth Exit

An old moth
the color of shingles
shuttered   and
fluttered its goodbye—

the glass that covered it
like a crumbling
artifact, I see,
was excess.

Down wings
powdered
its final perch
when the wind
lifted it away again,

its body
wedged
between the current
of a draft
and the living world.

Nocturnal Pine

With the windows open,
the trees keep us up.
Now that it is spring, most
of the pine needles
grow greener and fast and

s-sssh all through the night.
Most of their trunks
are still enough to be quiet

but one trunk, mildly
southwest of our bed

cracks and
groans like a door on a hinge in the rain,

creaks like a floor under
this warm rug of night—

in the most slight breeze,
sings like a swing on a chain.

Keeps us up isn't true—
husband sleeps soundly,
children sleep soundly
through the nocturnes
of the creaky pine.

Even the weeping cherry dries its eyes
for the night, its featherly leaves
only *shus*sing together,
and then, *shus*sing only if you listen hard.

I've heard the pine in the day,
and I've gone to see it, the sorrowful thing,
no branches, and nobody who hears
in the light of day—so

this nightly speech
and sough like old joints,

like hiss of pen on page.

Road Chickens

Chickens are packed like parcels
into the trailer that carries them—
crammed as shoes into boxes,
as feather pillows into their tight coops.

It is November, and north, and
at this stop light, they are both
weary, it seems, and near frozen.

Earthy yellow legs
pole through wire cages—

they cannot stand,
they cannot turn.

The edge chickens
are splashed, wind-blown,
deafened by the road—

I at once am compelled to
tell the children, *look, see the chickens*
and to shield their eyes.

September Ivy

Fall is the midnight of trees,
and they are elbow and celebration
by the side of the highway.

Some stand bare and alone,
unbending spindles so soon.

On others,
a lace of red leaves wraps
slim, bare trunks, their tips
dipped in gold and perfume.

They do not know—care?—that we
and a million others can see

and we do—we look with longing,

waiting to see if the vines will fall away,
if they will at last lift their roots
and embrace.

Yes, this is a poem about—
I won't kid myself—
they weren't perfect—
but at least they were round.

Now when I lie down,
they melt into my armpits
over the bank of my ribs,
asymmetric gelatin domes
sliding in the hot sun.

If I released them into the wild
they'd never come home,
but they wouldn't get far,

their noble faces
pointing haphazardly
as two broken compasses.

Poor dears, they'd wait
under the tree where I'd laid them down
to stare like empty plates into the sky,
wondering—as I have wondered—
where they have gone.

In Memory

When I'm gone,
please don't bring me
solar powered lights
or silk flowers
that spell out MOM
or patriotic ribbons
on the fourth of July,

for I will be busy
returning to the earth

and I won't have need
for the plastic stems and strands
that would, in the end,
inspire the production
of more of the same,
haunting us both,
collecting all of our dusts.

If you must lay something down,
bring me a sandwich
or water,

your handprint in the grass,

a note on a paper
that would
soon enough
catch up with me.

Neighbor Blessing

In your heaven, I hope
there are shining glass orbs
bouncing in the silver grass

swishing hostas to rinse over your legs
as you part their bedded green seas.

I hope you find a candle
casting from each window
and stained glass panes in the bathroom
so the colors may fall on you and bathe you
in the mornings.

May someone leave in your heaven
a box of free kittens
to float on the stony sidewalk
and charm the pedestrian shore.

And may you find a dried lobster
to adorn your gate
and a net to cast over the roving passers-by.

Nearsighted

The world is lighted
with charming surprises:

no animal has died in the road:
it is only a paper bag.

A speeding ticket
quickly becomes a love note
left by a love, and

why, no limbs
dangle from the trunk of that car,
it's only the sun catching the bumper just so.

Try it.

Azaleas and rhododendrons up close
become at any distance instead

low exploding fireworks
or hunched, inquisitive transients
out for the day
in their color-punched suits,

adjusting their glasses.

Memorable You

This night clings
to the vapor
of a fog so thick

you can hear it
light upon the street.

A collector,
I bring out my jar,
empty,

catch some night in it,

and write your name
on the lid.

Acknowledgments and Credits

May I express my appreciation to the editors of the publications where these poems have appeared, sometimes in a slightly different version:

"Summer Turning," in *Perigee* and in *Everything Stops and Listens* from OPA Press

"Pitcher," in Literary Mama

"Lillian Ode," "Moving Day," and "Rosary," in *Wooster Magazine*

"Nocturnal Pine," in *Adroit Journal*

"A Kind of Haunting," in *Lummox* and in *Connotation Press*

"Rainbow" in the anthology by Fearless Books, *The Light in Ordinary Things*

"Love Bugs" in *34th Parallel*

"After the Fish" in *About Place*

Many of the poems in this collection also appear in the 2011 chapbook from Finishing Line Press, *A Note on the Door.*

My heartfelt thanks also to my friends, colleagues, and mentors in the Ashland University MFA program, and friends elsewhere: your encouragement is an invaluable gift.

The Author

Born and raised on Cleveland's West Side, Jen Kindbom currently resides with her family in Wooster, Ohio. Jen studied at the College of Wooster and holds her MFA from Ashland University. She has taught English for a number of years to students in middle school, high school, and college.

Kindbom is passionate about unveiling poetry—a genre often described by students as mysterious, inaccessible, without objective meaning, and strictly rhyming—as "language concentrate," capable of communicating ideas and images in relatively few words.

www.ingramcontent.com/pod-product-compliance
Lightning Source LLC
Chambersburg PA
CBHW051348040426
42453CB00007B/473